Big Gold

Written by John Parsons

Illustrated by Gus Hunter

Contents Page

Nelson
an International Thomson Publishing company ITP®

Big Gold Mountain

With these characters ...

Ken Ng

Louie Chung

Sam Lee

"Soon, he woul

Setting the scene ...

Gold! That word inspired thousands of Chinese immigrants to come to Australia in the 1800s. After a month at sea, Ken, Louie and their fellow immigrants long for fresh food and clean water and are eager to start work on the gold-fields of 'Dai Gum San'—the Big Gold Mountain. But the path to riches has many problems. Ken and Louie have just a few years to pay back money borrowed from a rich landowner back home in China. How will they reach the gold-fields and who will pay the taxes no-one told them about? Will Ken and Louie find their fortune at Dai Gum San in time to pay their debts?

rrive at 'Dai Gum San' ..."

Chapter 1.

On board the ship, everyone was thinking the same thing: "At last!"

Feeling weary and nervous, but also excited, Ken Ng stood on the creaking wooden deck of the *Mary Christian*, along with fifty other Chinese immigrants. All eyes were fixed on the town that lay ahead of them.

A warm wind filled the ship's white sails, pushing the immigrants towards the new life that they had dreamed of for many months. Finally, their long journey from Canton in China to Australia was almost over.

When they had left Canton, the weather had been cold and rainy. As they travelled south, the rains had stopped. Gradually, the temperatures became hotter and the air more humid. Now, in January, Ken's face was covered in sweat. He was not used to such extreme temperatures.

Like all the other immigrants on board, Ken longed for fresh food and clean water. It had been a month since they had left the busy port of Canton. Since then, they had only eaten dried food and a small bowl of rice each day. Beneath the decks, where the immigrants had lived, eaten and slept, it was cramped, dark and smelly.

As Ken gazed at the land ahead, he felt sad at the thought of his family, far away in China. He wondered how long it would be before he saw his father, mother or sister again. Then he reminded himself why he had made this long, hard journey. The prospect of finding gold sent a shiver of excitement through his body. Soon, he would arrive at 'Dai Gum San': the Big Gold Mountain, or Bendigo, as it was known to the Australians.

“Soon, we will be rich,” whispered a voice at his side. Ken turned and smiled at his friend, Louie Chung. Louie was a short, strong man who always had a smile on his face.

Both Ken and Louie came from the same Chinese province, where most people were suffering hard times. On the journey from China, the two young men had become good friends, and often discussed how they would spend their fortunes.

"We will be able to repay the money we have borrowed for this journey. Better still, we will be able to send gold to our families. And, one day," winked Louie, "we will be able to return to China as the richest men in our province!"

Ken thought of the money that he had borrowed from a rich landowner in China. If he did not repay the money in five years, his family would have to give everything they owned to the landowner.

"If we work as hard as you dream, we will be very rich," Ken said. "For the sake of our families, I hope so."

Within an hour, the *Mary Christian* was tied up to a small wharf. The men on board waited quietly, as the ship rocked gently on the waves. There was a feeling of excitement all around. But that feeling was about to turn to gloom.

Two tall men, wearing official blue uniforms, climbed up the gangplank onto the ship's deck. After checking the other immigrants' arrival papers, one of the men finally reached Ken. Ken handed over the papers that said who he was and where he was from.

"Excuse me, sir," said Ken quietly. He was nervous about speaking English. "Will we be able to reach Bendigo before nightfall?"

The man that Ken was speaking to looked surprised. He frowned at Ken. Then he laughed harshly. He turned to the other man in uniform.

"This one wants to know if he will make it to Bendigo before nightfall!" he snorted rudely. The other man stared at Ken and rolled his eyes, before laughing too.

"Only if you run!" he said, chuckling loudly.

Ken did not understand why the men were laughing at him. He glanced at Louie, who was just as puzzled. The man handed back Ken's papers.

"You're in Adelaide," he said, narrowing his eyes. "Bendigo is another five hundred miles ... that way!" The man pointed towards the east.

Ken was shocked. Five hundred miles? He couldn't believe it. How was he going to reach Dai Gum San, with no money and no transport?

Chapter 2

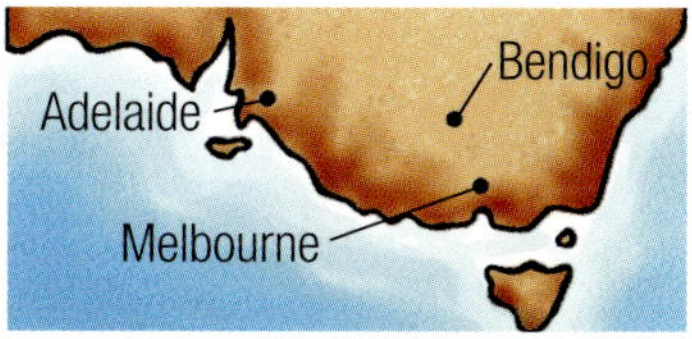

Ten minutes later, Ken, Louie and the other men stood on the wharf in disbelief. No-one had been told that their ship was going to land five-hundred miles from Bendigo. All the immigrants were talking frantically, with worried expressions on their faces. The people working on the wharf ignored them. They did not want to help the new immigrants. The captain of the *Mary Christian* refused to allow the men back onto the ship. They were stranded and alone, in a strange land.

Just as they were beginning to despair, a voice called out to them in their own language.

"You men! Pay attention!"

Ken, Louie and the other men were surprised to hear their own language. They stopped talking and turned to see who the voice belonged to.

Seated in the saddle of a huge brown stallion, a Chinese man dressed in expensive clothes looked down at the group of immigrants.

"I hear that you want to go to Dai Gum San," grinned the man. "Unfortunately, the government in this country does not like you," he continued.

"At Melbourne, the *nearest* port to Dai Gum San, you must pay a ten pound tax when you arrive."

The men were shocked. No-one had ten pounds.

It was more money than they could earn in a year in China. Everybody had already borrowed more money than they could afford to pay for their journey.

"Your captain has let you off in Adelaide. Here, you do not have to pay a tax. But," said the man, grinning again, "you have to walk a long, long way."

The man bowed his head, and smiled at the group.

"Fortunately, I am here to help you. My name is Sam Lee. I will guide you to Dai Gum San."

The men looked relieved and started to thank him excitedly, until Sam held up his hand and looked serious.

"All I ask in return is that you work for me for six months when you arrive," he said. "A small price to pay, I hope you will agree."

Ken and Louie looked at each other. The other men were silent. Everyone wondered if they could trust this man. But they all knew they had no choice. No-one knew where Bendigo was, or how to get there. The land around them was hot, strange and looked dangerous. Sam Lee was their only hope of survival.

Three days later, Ken was beginning to wonder if he had made a terrible mistake. His back ached from carrying food, water and a tent. After walking twenty miles each day, his feet were sore. Digging for water each night left his hands blistered and raw. And still, the group of Chinese immigrants had weeks of walking under the hot Australian sun ahead of them.

Sam Lee guided the men along the dusty, stone-filled road that seemed endless. Sometimes, when they passed a farm or a small township, he disappeared and returned with a sheep, which they roasted over a huge fire. In a tiny red book, he would write down how much the sheep had cost, and his wooden abacus would click as he worked out how much each man owed him for their food. Each day, the men owed Sam Lee more and more money.

Every night, they would set up camp and build a large, roaring fire. The men would sing sad songs about their homeland, play cards or simply dream about how rich they hoped to become. Each morning, before the sun had risen, the men would start their journey again, with Sam Lee riding ahead on his great brown stallion.

Ken dreaded the hot afternoons, when the temperature would reach thirty-five degrees, and the red dust from the road would dry his throat and his eyes until they felt like sandpaper. Then, at night, he would shiver under his thin blanket, as the temperature dropped to about four degrees.

"Soon, we will be rich," Louie kept saying, as they trudged closer and closer to Dai Gum San. Ken would always smile at his friend's cheerful attitude. "One day, you and I will have our own horses to ride around on."

"When we are the richest men in our province, we will visit each other on our own horses, Louie," laughed Ken.

At last, after twenty-five days of walking, the men arrived at Sam Lee's mining camp, at the edge of Dai Gum San. Their feelings of relief quickly turned into disappointment. It was not what they had expected.

Instead of finding a gleaming, golden mountain, they found a run-down group of wooden shacks. Mice and rats ran along the edges of the buildings. Strange birds, coloured pink and grey and red and blue, shrieked loudly from the trees that surrounded the buildings.

Exhausted miners rested on logs of wood outside their shacks. This was where Sam Lee's men worked off their debt to him. This was to be their home for the next six months.

Sam showed the men into a ramshackle hut, and told them to be ready at dawn for work. Ken was too tired to eat the small amount of rice that Sam had left them. All he wanted to do was collapse into the tiny wooden bunk that was his bed.

"At last," he thought, as he drifted into a deep sleep. "At last, there will be no more travelling."

Chapter 3.

The next morning, Ken and Louie stood at the front of the group of new arrivals, eager to start work in the gold-fields.

"The quicker we work, the faster we pay off the money we owe," whispered Louie, winking.

Ken smiled at him, but secretly, he was worried. He owed money to the rich landowner back in China. He owed Sam Lee money for food. By promising to work for him for six months, Ken knew it was going to be an awfully long time before he saw any gold of his own. He was amazed at how Louie could always be so cheerful.

Just then, they turned around to see Sam Lee standing before them.

"I have some more information for you," he said, grinning. Ken started to feel worried. On the long walk from Adelaide to Bendigo, Ken had learned that whenever Sam Lee grinned, it meant that there was trouble ahead.

"The Australian government demands that you pay four pounds a year as a residence tax. If you want to live here, you must pay the four pounds today."

The men groaned. No-one had been told about these taxes before they left Canton. And everyone realised what Sam Lee was about to suggest.

"Fortunately, I have already paid this tax for all of you," said Sam. "And the good news is that I do not wish you to repay the money. All you need to do is to work for me for another three months after your *first* six months is completed."

Sam looked around the silent group. Ken stared at the dusty ground. He could not complain. He began to feel trapped and depressed. He began to worry that he would never be rich.

Everyone else was too scared to say anything, either, so Sam Lee clapped his hands.

"No-one is complaining, so let's start work immediately."

For the next nine months, Ken, Louie and the other men worked from dawn until nightfall. The Chinese gold miners were only allowed to work on the left-over diggings, after the European miners had taken away most of the gold. The day was long and the work was hard. Ken's body ached at the end of every day. He worked, ate and slept. There was no time for anything else, except wondering how his family was, and whether he would ever be able to repay the money he owed.

The hot summer days turned into autumn, and then winter. Snow lay on the ground all around the camp. Ken and Louie worked on a machine called a sluice. They shovelled tonnes of mud and soil and stone into one end of a long wooden trough that had water running through it. Along the bottom of the sluice were hundreds of ridges. As the mud and soil was carried along by the water, the heavy gold dust sank to the bottom of the sluice and collected along the ridges.

Every few hours, they rested on their shovels and watched Sam Lee carefully collecting the tiny specks of gold.

They watched as Sam Lee grinned and walked away with the results of their hard work.

Ken felt exhausted, and even Louie was less cheerful.

“Only a few more weeks, and we’ll be able to keep the gold dust for ourselves,” Louie would whisper. “Our backs won’t hurt as much and our hands won’t feel as frozen when it is *our* gold dust.”

Ken nodded. But he knew it might take years before he and Louie could repay the money they had borrowed. Only then would the gold dust they worked so hard to discover be theirs to keep.

The men from Sam Lee's camp rarely went into the town of Bendigo. Some of the Europeans stared at them suspiciously, and some called them insulting names. Others laughed at the clothes they wore and the food they wanted to eat. Ken and Louie did not understand why the Europeans did not like them. They kept out of trouble, and did not do anything to upset the Europeans.

Then, one day, when Louie and Ken were getting ready to celebrate the end of their nine months' work for Sam Lee, something unexpected happened.

Chapter 4.

Ken and Louie had finished their shovelling for the day, and were cleaning their tools in the dirty stream beside their sluice.

Suddenly, Ken saw Sam Lee's boots standing in front of him. Ken looked up, expecting to see Sam smile and announce some more bad news. Instead, Sam Lee clutched something in his hand. He looked very sad.

"Louie Chung," he said gently. "I have some bad news."

Louie slowly put down his shovel and turned to face Sam Lee.

"I received this letter for you this morning. I am very sorry." Sam offered Louie the letter, which was folded inside a tiny red envelope.

Louie looked embarrassed. "Sam Lee, please read the letter to me."

Sam nodded and opened the envelope.

"Dear brother Louie, there has been a terrible outbreak of smallpox in our province and our father is very ill," he read. "By the time you receive this, it may be too late. You must come home immediately to look after our mother, who is too old to work, and our grandmother, who is also very ill. Without you, we will have no money and no food. Our situation is very bad. We are depending on you to help us. Please hurry. Your loving sister, Mae."

Sam Lee shook his head, and handed Louie the letter.

"I really am very sorry," he said.

"Thank you, Sam Lee," said Louie sadly. For once, the smile was gone from his face. He looked at the ground.

"I do not know what to do. I must go home," he said anxiously. "I cannot let my family starve. But I have no money to pay for a ship. And I still owe a lot of money for my trip out here."

For the first time in almost a year, Ken saw his friend looking desperately worried. He thought about how they were almost free from Sam Lee.

He thought about how he was almost ready to start paying back the money he owed the rich landowner in China. He thought about his friend's terrible bad luck. He knew what he must do.

"I will help you, Louie. Go and pack your belongings. You must leave on the next ship."

Chapter 5.

Ken worked on Sam Lee's sluice for another two years to repay the money he borrowed to buy Louie's fare home. He missed Louie's cheerful smile and his kindness. He missed talking about the things that they would do together when they were rich. But Sam Lee had been so impressed by Ken's act of friendship that, each week, he allowed him to keep a tiny amount of the gold dust that he collected in his sluice. Slowly, Ken saved up enough gold dust to start paying back the money he owed to the landowner in China.

After two years, Ken asked Sam Lee if he could keep working for him, in return for half the gold he collected. Sam Lee agreed, and Ken gradually began to save up more and more gold dust. He sent gold back to China, to his family and to the landowner. He kept a small portion for himself, knowing that one day, he would need to buy his own sluice.

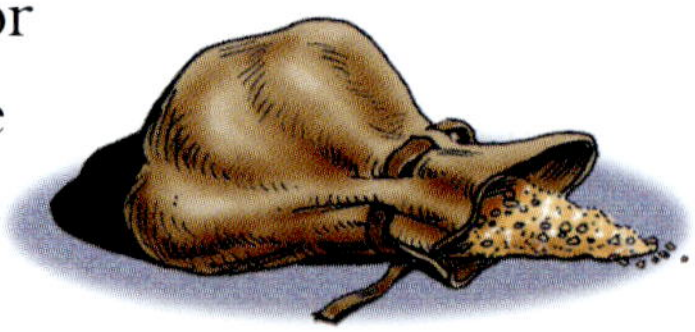

Four years after his arrival in Adelaide, Ken had shovelled countless tonnes of mud and dirt through Sam Lee's sluice. His body was hard and tough. His skin was dark from the sun. His hands no longer blistered, and his back no longer ached. He still missed Louie and his family, but he had reached his goal. He had enough gold dust saved up to buy his own sluice.

Almost a year later, one spring day in 1862, five years after his long, hot, dusty walk from Adelaide to Bendigo, Ken Ng looked very different from the new immigrant who had arrived in this strange country so long ago.

He walked back from the town, along the same dusty, red path that he had walked so many times in the past year. Every week, since building his own sluice, he had sent some of his gold dust back to China, and sold the rest of it to get money for food. But today, he not only looked different from the new immigrant he had once been. Something else had changed.

Ken looked around at his small wooden house, at his few possessions and at his sluice. He looked up at the bright blue sky. He looked at the gum trees that surrounded him, and listened to the calls of the rosellas and the galahs flying overhead. Then he smiled. After five long, hard years, he had paid back all the money he had borrowed.

At last, he thought to himself. At last, I do not owe anybody anything.

At last, I am a free man!

During the 1800s, there were many gold discoveries in Australia, New Zealand and in California, in the United States. Many thousands of Chinese workers travelled to these lands in the hope of a better life for themselves and for their families back home in China.

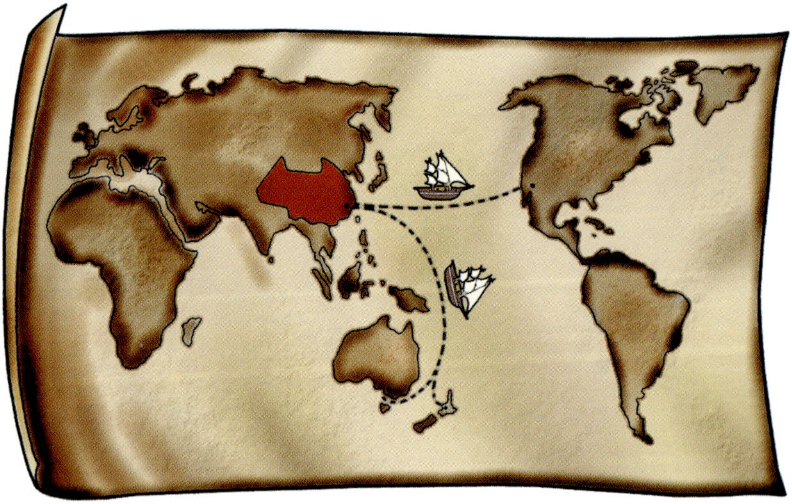

They found conditions very hard, and many immigrants died on the journey to their new lands. Once they were in their new lands, they often found that the governments there charged them many unfair taxes, and they were not always treated well by the other people who lived there.

Most Chinese goldminers worked very hard, paying off the money they owed back in China, and sending gold home to help their families. During 1857, almost 6 tonnes, or 6,000 kilograms, of gold was shipped from Australia to China by goldminers.

Eventually, however, the gold in each of the places where the Chinese settled started to run out. Often, the Chinese people were not allowed to work at other jobs, and many were forced to return home. Some remained, and started their own businesses or worked in jobs that others would not do, like growing vegetables or cleaning. In some places, it took over a hundred years before people realised what a valuable contribution the Chinese immigrants had made, and were making, to the local communities.

"Gold!"

The big gold mountain:
An unforgiving dragon,
Consuming your dreams.